Shadows of the
BIG FOUR

R. J. BLENKINSOP

© **1975** Oxford Publishing Co.

SBN 902888 61 7

Set, printed and bound in the City of Oxford
Plates by Oxford Litho Plates

Published by:
Oxford Publishing Co.
8 The Roundway
Risinghurst
Oxford

PREFACE

Since the publication of my series of books on the 'Great Western', I have received numerous letters from enthusiasts asking if I could produce a book covering the other regions of British Rail. Being completely immune from any partisan feelings, I had always tried to explore other routes with different engines but this of course relied on travelling further afield.

This book is made up of almost equal numbers of photographs from each region and we hope to continue with further volumes at a later date.

I am sure if one studies the collection of any railway photographer, one will find that the subject matter is very bound up with his domestic situation and in my case this is certainly so. After leaving school in 1948, I started taking photographs with a variety of box cameras until my 21st birthday in 1951 when I was given a No. 120 size folding camera of reasonable quality which was responsible for the first fifty pictures in this book. Thereafter I used a large converted press camera, still taking No. 120 film.

In the early 1950's I had a girl friend who lived in Cheshire and worked in London, which involved me in a considerable amount of travelling in both directions. This accounts for London, Liverpool and Chester being well represented in my books. We were married in 1955 which accounted for a change in the geographical location and during holidays or 'days off' I managed to get around to other places.

On looking through these pictures I realise just how lucky I was to have seen so much and indeed had transport to do so. My first car was a very worn out Austin Seven Ruby Saloon which ran a big end on the way back from London. I was therefore stranded at Watford and in the process took picture No. 22 while I awaited a train back home.

As you will read in the captions, we had a honeymoon in the Channel Islands as I thought it was only fair to spend this time away from railways and a careful check established that the Jersey railways were lifted. However, the journey home produced a good collection of pictures which more than compensated for the two weeks of starvation!

I was exceedingly lucky to get both pictures 30 and 31 as those of you who know the bridge from which the pictures were taken can imagine the problem of scaling the parapet and pointing a camera downwards without falling over.

Having now an active interest in the Traction Engine Movement, I recall the journey back home after taking picture No. 36 as I came face to face with two Fowler ploughing engines round a sharp corner near Uppingham. This chance meeting has sparked off a new interest which I can recommend to any steam engine enthusiast. Incidentally the Fowlers were out 'on contract' and happily are now in preservation.

The pictures taken at Gloucester came to be taken as No. 4056 Princess Margaret had just completed its last major overhaul at Swindon, and after telephoning the works I discovered it was working the running in turn from Swindon to Gloucester. While awaiting its arrival, I spent a useful two hours at Tramway Junction which was such a splendid place for watching the trains go by.

To put these photographs together in chronological order, it has needed much research to jog my memory into action. This has given me great satisfaction, which will be all the greater if this book revives similar memories for you.

1   Leamington Spa Avenue Station in the middle of a winter morning, showing one of F.W. Webb's 2-4-2T of 1890 vintage with an Auto-train for Rugby. Apart from the edge of the platform there is no trace left of this scene today. The ornate supporting brackets for the station roof are worthy of study.

29 December 1951

2 The track layout today has been very much simplified with a single line branching off to Stratford-on-Avon on the left. No. 6005 **King George II** approaches Hatton Station with the 11.35 Wolverhampton-Paddington and an L.M.S. coach leading, with the engine in blue livery. In the up loop a freight train is just visible hauled by ex-works R.O.D. No. 3033.

30 January 1952

3 This is a sight to thrill L.N.W.R. enthusiasts as G2a Class 0-8-0 No. 49181 accelerates away from Harbury Cement Works after the long drag up from Leamington. It was working a Nuneaton-Banbury coal train and makes a magnificent sight as the smoke hangs under the bridge on a brilliant winter morning.

4   You will notice the flat bottom track going down the Lickey incline to Bromsgrove as a Midland 0-6-0 No. 43210 climbs the 1 in 37 banked by an 0-6-0 tank engine in the rear. This was taken on a very dull day and just before the fireman got to work with the shovel. There was another photographer further up the hill who won a competition in 'Trains Illustrated' with his picture of this same freight train.

12 April 1952

5   I was fortunate living at Leamington as all the Big Four were close at hand. The Great Central provided my ex-L.N.E.R. motive power and in this case it is No. 60059 **Tracery** climbing past Staverton Road signal box with the up *Master Cutler* from Sheffield to Marylebone. This named train started running during the 1951 Festival of Britain.

19 April 1952

6 You may recall the British Industries Fair which was held at Castle Bromwich not far from the new National Exhibition Centre now under construction. A special was run each day from Euston in the morning and this picture is the return train in the evening. No. 45669 **Fisher** pilots class 5 No. 45064 past Cathiron with a 15-coach load, both engines being in black livery.

15 May 1952

7 Another picture on the Great Central showing the afternoon down *South Yorkshireman* approaching Staverton Road signal box. You will notice the sides of the cutting are comparatively shallow, a Board of Trade requirement when this line was built. No. 60103 **Flying Scotsman** has a rake of the latest L.N.E.R. steel coaches.

24 May 1952

8 Turning around from the previous picture, class O1 2-8-0 No. 63803 climbs slowly up the hill towards Woodford. Both the crew are looking out on this warm summer evening and the fireman has obviously been filling up the box judging by what is coming out of the chimney!

24 May 1952

9 Passing the recently demolished L.N.E.R. signal box at Kenilworth Junction is class 5 No. 44833 with the 07.16 (S.O.) Leamington-Llandudno which started as empty stock, from Long Itchington. You will notice the signalman at his window with the staff hanging from his hand which will allow the train to proceed on the single line to Coventry. The reflecting object seen through the forward cab window is a new bucket hanging on the front of the tender.

28 June 1952

11 Another Stephenson Locomotive Society special which started from Cardiff and made a tour of the more obscure lines in the Welsh valleys. 0-6-0PT No. 6423 stands in Llantrisant station with two 70' trailers, the nearest being No. 32 built in 1906.

12 July 1952

10 Engines of the 'Star' class were difficult to find in the Midlands but a number could be seen on the Swindon line in 1952. Near Wantage and on its way up to London is No. 4062 **Malmesbury Abbey** with elbow steam pipes. Taken with the sun in the west late in the evening it could not be a more difficult picture to print, but nevertheless there is movement and a blurred background to give an impression of speed.

5 July 1952

12 This picture is included for the 'environmentalists' to show what Paddington could be like but in fact seldom was so. The fireman of No. 5051 **Earl Bathurst** seems to have overdone things as the driver awaits departure from No. 2 platform. A 'Britannia' is visible in the background blowing off steam on this dull, dark morning.

4 October 1952

13 I must have travelled onto Oxford by train as this picture shows the fireman involved in uncoupling No. 34110 **66 Squadron** from a through train with engine change at Oxford. Of interest today is the leather strap for adjusting the window and the wooden slats on the carriage roof felting.

4 October 1952

14 A scene familiar to Midlanders and those who frequented Birmingham New Street station. It seems strange to look at this picture and compare it with today's smooth operation. L.M.S. compounds with Stanier chimneys Nos. 41046 and 41195 are seen complete with the Midland deep buffer beam, black at the top and vermillion below.
25 October 1952

15 The 10.15 Paddington-Wolverhampton climbs Hatton Bank on a sunny winter morning behind No. 6904 **Charfield Hall** in Great Western livery with coat of arms on the tender and No. 5960 **Saint Edmund Hall**, newly painted in black but running with a green tender.
28 February 1953

16 Another class O1 2-8-0 No. 63596 on the Great Central at Loughborough, crossing the Midland main line, the bridge being in the foreground. This is a down freight train on a dull day which I spent switching from the Great Central to the Midland, and back depending on the state of the signals!
21 March 1953

17 The preservationists of the Main Line Steam Trust will appreciate this as it shows B1 No. 61160 leaving Loughborough Great Central station with the up *South Yorkshireman*. Mainly L.N.E.R. teak stock but some already painted in that frightful cream and red.
21 March 1953

18 Fairburn 2-6-4T No. 42160 leaves Loughborough Midland station with a Nottingham-Leicester stopping train and an L.N.W.R. 0-8-0 plods on slowly south with a freight train with the driver much exposed to the east wind. The Great Central can be seen crossing in the background.

21 March 1953

19 In fact I had no intention of taking this picture with the engine going away, but when a wall of water and spray approaches at 60 m.p.h. like this one did there is no alternative. Goring Troughs at its wettest with No. 5940 **Whitbourne Hall** on its way from Paddington to Swindon.

7 April 1953

20 Cholsey and Moulsford station looking towards Reading with 'West Country' Pacific No. 34094 **Mortehoe** crossing from the down fast to the relief line as it would be taking the east avoiding line at Didcot to Oxford for a change of engines.

7 April 1953

21 At the other end of the station was Dean Goods 0-6-0 No. 2532 shunting wagons from the Wallingford branch. This engine built in 1897 was on loan to the Manchester and Milford Railway in 1906 and ran as their No. 10. It was one of the last of the class to be withdrawn in 1954 and judging by the state of the chimney was in a sorry state. The birds were building their nests high in the trees so it must have been a good summer in Coronation Year!

7 April 1953

22 This is a view looking north east at Watford station on a Sunday evening with No. 46129 **The Scottish Horse** having just pulled in with a train from Euston. Watford shed is in the background with quite a variety of motive power. The L.N.W.R. water column shows up clearly in the foreground.

19 April 1953

23 At Castle Bromwich station B1 No. 61190 runs in with a stopping train for Birmingham New Street. This was another British Industries Fair occasion, the exhibition buildings being shown on the left where skyscraper flats now abound. Notice the electric headlamps with oil lamps mounted on the top, and there is also a freight train approaching on the right.

24 Class T9 4-4-0 No. 30285 stands at Andover station gently blowing off steam before leaving for Eastleigh where it was shedded. I am sorry the coupling rods are up inside the splashers but it is difficult to arrange for them to be visible on every occasion!

14 June 1953

25 A well-known view looking towards Waterloo with Wimbledon station in the background and yard on the right. There is a convenient footpath on the left leading down to a footbridge across the tracks. 'King Arthur' No. 30789 **Sir Guy** heads south into the high midday sun.

20 June 1953

26 All 0-6-0 tender engines in Wimbledon Yard. On the left is No.
30694 Class 700 and in the centre is No. 30572, with No. 32524 on
the right. Judging by the lack of activity in the picture it must have
been the lunch hour!

20 June 1953

27 This is possibly a Waterloo-Lymington train emerging from under the
shops at Wimbledon station hauled by class L12 4-4-0 No. 30434.
20 June 1953

28 No. 30453 **King Arthur** approaches Wimbledon with a southbound train in the upper photograph and later the same day I travelled back into London and walked over the Thames to Charing Cross Station. Two 'Schools' class engines, both with standard chimney fortunately, are seen at the end of the platforms. No. 30935 **Sevenoaks** arrives
29 while No. 30912 **Downside** waits to leave with a train for Tunbridge Wells.

20 June 1953

30 Camden Bank outside Euston early in the morning. No. 46237 **City of Bristol** has a sleeping car train from Glasgow while an 8F 2-8-0 takes empty 12-wheel sleeping cars back to Willesden for servicing. In the background an 0-6-0T shunts stock for the down *Red Rose* Euston-Liverpool. Note the L.N.W.R. signal, the steam from the tender coal pusher, and the remains of streamlining on the top of the smokebox.

25 July 1953

31 This is undoubtedly one of my best pictures, looking down Camden Bank into Euston which is just out of the picture on the left. No. 45721 **Impregnable** has a push at the back of the train by an 0-6-0T and above the **Jubilee** are two more 0-6-0T's with a rebuilt **Royal Scot** attached to its train which was to form the down 'Irish Mail'. You will also notice the enormous carriage shed in the background and an '8F' on the left.

25 July 1953

32 No medals for guessing this location but I do recommend that you study carefully the external condition of No. 60028 **Walter K. Whigham** as it stands at Kings Cross awaiting departure with the down *Elizabethan*. Notice the burnished buffers, cylinder covers and all the valve gear.

33 The down **Royal Scot** emerges from Primrose Hill tunnel and into the closed South Hampstead station. The Great Central out of Marylebone crosses just above the tunnel mouth and No. 46224 **Princess Alexandra** is in green livery with the latest headboard. Those 'Virol' advertisements must have adorned railway property far and wide.

34 I spent a day at Rhyl on the main Chester-Holyhead line and this picture shows a train entering the station from Llandudno comprising L.N.E.R. stock with class 5's No. 44714 and 45195. Of interest is the large bell on the side of the L.N.W.R. signal box above the steam dome of the first engine.

35 Standing beside the water tank at Peterborough is K3 2-6-0 No. 61821 having its tender replenished. There appears to be a crew of three but perhaps the man pointing his hand came off another engine. The design of the water column is interesting with its operating lever.

20 September 1952

36

The reason for going to Peterborough was to see a special train from London to Doncaster for the Centenary Celebrations of the works. For this occasion two Ivatt 'Atlantics' were removed from York museum and subsequently worked a number of special trains before going back to the museum. Both these pictures were taken from the first road bridge to the north of Peterborough station which required dashing across the busy road and winding on at the same time. It was again one of those lucky occasions when the sun was not wanted as it was immediately behind the train and it would have ruined the picture had it been shining. Peterborough Cathedral shows up clearly on the skyline with the brickwork chimneys in the distance.

20 September 1953

37

38 Standing in the up platform at Coventry Station with a local train to Rugby is compound 4-4-0 No. 41163. This picture gives a good impression of the old station with its two platforms and fast lines in the middle. Note the ornate cast brackets for supporting the roof.

24 September 1953

39 The first express out of Worcester in the morning carried the 260 reporting numbers and it is shown here entering Paddington under steam, probably having been held by signals at the entrance to the station. No. 5063 **Earl Baldwin** is the 'Castle' class engine hauling this train with more 'Virol' advertising in the background.

26 September 1953

40 A delightful sight at Gloucester standing between the two stations, 0-4-4T No. 58071 built by Neilson & Co. in 1883 for the Midland Railway. It retained the Johnson Class C round top boiler and was one of ten fitted with condensing equipment for working the Metropolitan widened lines. Note the elegant shape of this engine with its Salter safety valves as it awaits duty on a foggy November morning.
18 November 1953

41 A ray of sunshine slants through the fog to show a busy scene just outside Gloucester. The Great Western shed is on the right with an 0-4-2T on the turntable. On the left 0-6-0 class 4F No. 44567 shunts wagons in the sidings outside Eastgate station. Jinty 0-6-0 No. 47607 is on the left and the variety of signals is a pleasure to study.
18 November 1953

42 This photograph shows the tramway crossing at the back of the Great Western Gloucester shed. It is a crossing widely known for its disruption to road traffic and the fantastic variety of motive power from many railways which have used the Midland and Great Western lines. No. 6918 **Sandon Hall** still in Great Western livery has just left Gloucester Central station and is passing the crossing keeper's hut.

18 November 1953

43 I have included this picture as it shows wrong line working on a Sunday between Leamington and Warwick. The train is the 11.10 Paddington-Birkenhead hauled by No. 6018 **King Henry VI** which was the first of the 'Kings' I saw to be repainted green after their few years in blue which somehow did not suit them and looked terrible when dirty.

14 February 1954

44

It makes one wonder at which end of the engine was fitted the water scoop as No. 4977 **Watcombe Hall** passes over Lapworth troughs with an up freight. I assume it is the A.T.C. equipment creating all the spray the like of which I have never seen before or since.
20 February 1954

45

The exhaust from No. 6844 **Penhydd Grange** blackens the sky as it approaches Stratton St. Margaret with a down freight. Shedded at Llanelly it was probably on its way back to South Wales.
6 March 1954

46 Both drivers are leaning out of their cabs as they emerge from Kilsby Tunnel into the bright sunshine with a Wolverhampton-Euston express. There was a P.W. slack in operation at that time so class 5 No. 45310 and No. 45641 **Sandwich** are moving slowly over the newly laid and unballasted track.

27 March 1954

47 This was quite a lucky shot just to the south of Rugby Great Central station, showing A3 'Pacific' No. 60050 **Persimmon** accelerating down the hill with the up *Master Cutler.* K3 2-6-0 No. 61980 has a freight from Woodford on its way north with the steam from both engines showing up clearly on a lovely spring morning.

27 March 1954

48 My old friend the 11.35 Wolverhampton-Paddington in Harbury cutting hauled by No. 6016 **King Edward V**. This is a somewhat unusual view as the trees and bushes had just been cut down on the west embankment. By the end of the year they had grown up again and have never been cut since, making photography impossible.

27 March 1954

49 The down *Pembroke Coast Express* approaches Twyford with tall chimneyed No. 5089 **Westminster Abbey.** The old type of aluminium headboard is carried and the train comprises a set of Great Western coaches.

19 April 1954

PASSENGERS ARE REQUESTED TO CROSS THE LINE BY THE BRIDGE

30862

50

To achieve a reasonable quota of pictures I had to cheat a little and use the through trains which had Southern motive power southwards from Oxford. No. 30862 **Lord Collingwood** has just come off Reading West curve and enters the station where it will stop. The new British Rail coaches contrast with the rather 'worse for wear' Great Western signals.

19 April 1954

51

Totally unexpected, this excursion has just passed through Coventry station on its way to Birmingham. B1 No. 61138 looks spick and span with its set of North Eastern stock and this view is of interest now that the scene has changed so much due to electrification. They must have had fun taking down that tall L.N.W.R. signal!

27 May 1954

52 This is Hatton Bank but not a view often seen in pictures. My open Morris Minor stands on the bridge so it must have been a warm evening as No. 5972 **Olton Hall** travels onto Warwick with a semi-fast from Birmingham Snow Hill. I think the engine came from Tyseley and is in black livery.

4 June 1954

53 The next five pictures were all taken at Worting junction just to the south of Basingstoke where the line to Salisbury and the west leaves the main line from Waterloo to Bournemouth. No. 30457 **Sir Bedivere** comes round the curve and under the flyover on its way to Salisbury. What an exciting change it was to see these handsome engines and green coaches.

7 June 1954

54 On its way up to London from Exeter is No. 35003 **Royal Mail** of the 'Merchant Navy' class.

7 June 1954

55 And now coming down from Waterloo past the flyover and onto Micheldever is 'West Country' Pacific No. 34020 **Seaton**. These were always difficult engines to photograph unless the sun was shining on to the smokebox as the smoke deflectors and top cowling invariably caused nasty shadows on the front.

7 June 1954

56 This one is taken from the flyover looking west as an up train from Salisbury approaches behind No. 30450 **Sir Kay**.

7 June 1954

57 The final picture at Battledown flyover shows an up train from Bournemouth behind 'West Country' Pacific No. 34093 **Saunton**. You notice the magnificent sky and the banks of cloud coming up from the south west. As luck would have it the clouds stayed on either side of the sun for most of the morning.

7 June 1954

58 On my way home I stopped at the south end of Cholsey cutting to see yet another through train from the north which picked up a Southern engine at Oxford. In this case it is No. 30742 **Camelot**.
7 June 1954

59 Next day was stormy but justified this picture of 2-6-2T No. 5161 coming up the last mile to Leamington Spa with a pick up freight which would probably go straight into the goods yard. The engine was shedded at Leamington and is still in Great Western livery.
8 June 1954

60 Waterloo station on a dull day with 'Merchant Navy' class Pacific No. 35011 **General Steam Navigation** awaiting the "right away" with the down *Bournemouth Belle*. Of all the titled trains the *Belle* always gave me the greatest thrill as it swept by with its set of Pullman cars and attendants in their smart uniform.

31 July 1954

61 London commuters may recognise this location with West Hampstead tube station on the right. No. 60054 **Prince of Wales** is about to start the final part of its journey through the tunnels down the hill to Marylebone with the up *Master Cutler*. The engine was in blue livery.

2 August 1954

62 Hatfield was not far out of my way when returning home to Leamington and I stopped at the sweeping curve to the south of the station. No. 60149 **Amadis** has an up express while V2 No. 60867 passes by in the opposite direction. Although very much a dull weather photograph with two dirty engines, it is still a view very much part of the everyday running of a railway.

63 'Britannia' Pacific No. 70045 was unnamed when this picture was taken as it passes the Point of Air on the North Wales main line with the 15-coach down 'Irish Mail'. You will notice the coal is well down in the tender, and just visible shunting on the right is Lancashire and Yorkshire 0-6-0 No. 52356.

64 Here we have another atmospheric offering as 2-8-2T No. 7212 toils up Campden Bank with a loaded up coal train shortly after leaving Honeybourne. I was on my way to Devon for a quick weekend of photography and from the car noticed the smoke in the distance so stopped and quickly found a suitable spot by the roadside.

20 August 1954

65 No. 45738 **Samson** passes Radford Brewery with a diverted Sunday Wolverhampton-Euston express. The Leamington-Rugby line is now removed here and Radford Brewery demolished and replaced by the offices of the East Midlands Electricity Board. The Thornley family who owned the brewery were great users of the famous Foden steam wagon for delivery of their beer but before my time I'm afraid.

66 I have included this picture as it shows an old signalman friend of mine at Southam Road and Harbury signal box together with his bicycle which was the standard form of local transport in those days. A rather grubby 'King' No. 6014 **King Henry VII** passes by with an up express from Wolverhampton. The scene today is very different with just two main lines, and no sidings, station or signal box.

20 February 1955

67 A classic train which always had 6P or 7P motive power. It left Leamington Avenue station at 07.55 as a stopping train to Birmingham where it became an express on to Liverpool. The return working arrived in Leamington in the early hours of the morning. This picture shows it rounding the curve at Kenilworth Junction, taking the Berkswell line. 'Royal Scot' No. 46151 **The Royal Horse Guardsman** produces a realistic shadow on the embankment as its exhaust billows forth on a cold morning.

68 Southern engines were not fitted with water pick-up equipment as the Southern Railway did not really require water troughs due to lack of long non-stop runs. 'Lord Nelson' class 4-6-0 No. 30861 **Lorn Anson** passes over Goring troughs on its way from Reading to Oxford.

2 April 1955

69   Ian Allan Ltd. ran a special from Paddington-Bristol-Birmingham and back to London and No. 7017 **G.J. Churchward** hauled the train to Bristol and Birmingham. It was routed on the Midland line up the Lickey incline. This picture shows the famous 0-10-0 No. 58100 banking the train with the 'Coronation' beaver tail observation car at the rear of the train.

16 April 1955

70 A Stanier 'Pacific' was loaned to the Western Region for trials and comparison with the 'King' class engines of the Great Western. The engine selected was No. 46237 **City of Bristol** and, before working the trials proper with Dynamometer car on the Plymouth run, it spent a few days coming down to Birmingham. Here it is passing Hatton North Junction with the 09.10 Paddington-Birkenhead.

27 April 1955

71 The driver is seated peering through the cab front window of No. 6005 **King George II** as it descends Hatton Bank with the 15.00 Birmingham Snow Hill-Paddington. The tender top is interesting, covered with coal or a mixture of coal and water slopping around in the back.

18 June 1955

moon in Jersey. The boat express from Southampton to Waterloo was hauled by No. 30864 **Sir Martin Frobisher** and is shown in the entrance to the customs house where the rest of the train was stabled. Class USA 0-6-0T No. 30063 stands on the left of the picture.
9 July 1955

73 **Sir Martin Frobisher** pulls slowly out of Southampton Docks across the main road and on its way to Waterloo through the terminus station. The beautiful face of the South Western Hotel shows up clearly in the bright afternoon sunshine.
9 July 1955

74 Both these pictures were taken at speed from the carriage window. Eastleigh shed has a varied selection of motive power on display, and I think it is best for you to test your powers of recognition. Numbers are hardly legible but the two 'King Arthurs' on the right are No. 30767 **Sir Valence** and No. 30764 **Sir Gawain**.

9 July 1955

75 I cannot make up my mind if an M7 0-4-4T is male or female. Someone has certainly made up their mind as "Pat" appears quite clearly on the front of the smoke box. No. 30378 is running into Eastleigh with a stopping train from Winchester.

9 July 1955

76 We had to change at Basingstoke for the journey onto Leamington and there was time to take a few pictures. Running into Basingstoke from the Reading line is class U 2-6-0 No. 31630 with a set of vintage coaches.

9 July 1955

77 Turning round from the previous picture my camera was pointing at 'Remembrance' class 4-6-0 No. 32330 **Cudworth.** This engine, one of a small class of seven was a rebuild from L. Billington's 'L' class 4-6-4T's built between 1914 and 1922.

9 July 1955

78 No. 45544, an unnamed member of the 'Patriot' class, is seen backing out of Liverpool Lime Street station past the usual crowd of engine spotters who now have electrics and diesels to fill their notebooks.

16 July 1955

79 Looking very smart in its new coat of paint, class C14 4-4-2T No. 67442 stands in Neston North station with a train for Wrexham. Judging by the number of heads appearing from the window there were quite a number of people travelling on this Sunday morning. The station architecture is worthy of note together with the water column.

80 Two studies of class N5 0-6-2T in the Wirral. No. 69362 leaves Burton Point with a train for Wrexham.
3 September 1955

81 and in the lower photograph No. 69267 starts away from Chester Northgate station now closed and demolished.
3 September 1955

82　By Chester golf course in the evening the up 'Irish Mail' approaches behind 'Britannia' Pacific No. 70046 while 'Class 5' No. 45002 accelerates out of the cutting on its way along the North Wales coast.

3 September 1955

83　There seems to be quite a mixture here in Great Western territory at Aynho water troughs, where a culvert bridge is being replaced over the troughs. It was single line Sunday working and the two 'Directors' class D11 4-4-0 No. 62666 **Zeebrugge** and No. 62667 **Somme** are working a special train to the Farnborough Air display.

11 September 1955

84 The scene is Shrewsbury Great Western shed with visiting class T9 4-4-0 No. 30304 being prepared for the Tallylyn Railway Preservation Society special which it worked to Towyn together with 'Dukedog' 4-4-0 No. 9027 coming on at Welshpool.

24 September 1955

85 A class G2 0-8-0 climbs up to Runcorn bridge with an up freight on the main Liverpool-London line, now of course electrified. I seem to recall that this picture was taken from the transporter bridge on one of my numerous journeys across while hoping a train would appear.

15 October 1955

86 The weather was miserable on every Saturday while the ''King crisis'' was on; you may remember they were all withdrawn after faults appearing in bogies and main frames. In this picture No. 46254 **City of Stoke-on-Trent** leaves Leamington with the 09.10 Paddington-Birkenhead. For the record there were four Stanier 'Pacifics' on loan, namely Nos. 46207/10 and 46254/7.

28 January 1956

87 A real example of push and pull with 0-4-2T No. 1416 in the middle heading into Chester and crossing the River Dee with the race course on the right. A freight train is disappearing on the up main line, and coming this way on the down relief a Great Western 'Hall' is towing a 'Mogul' and a British Rail standard class 5 No. 73099.

10 March 1956

89 The 'King' class had now all returned back in service and No. 6007 **King William III** is shown on the climb up to Fenny Compton with the 15.00 Birmingham-Paddington. The exact location is just short of the earth works which were begun and of course never finished to take the Great Western line through Southam.

2 April 1956

88 The Royal train leaves Coventry after H.M. The Queen had laid the foundation stone for the new Coventry Cathedral. Class 5's No. 44829 and No. 44833 pass Humber Road signal box with the spire of the old Cathedral visible on the right. The first coach was part of the L.N.W.R. 'Royal train' built at Wolverton and the remaining coaches are the 1941 stock.

23 March 1956

90 The two sides of Catesby tunnel are shown in these two pictures. Class O1 2-8-0 No. 63887 has a down freight from Woodford about 1 mile north of the tunnel which can just be seen above the platelayer's hut.

12 May 1956

91 Believed to be the first time a Pullman car train had worked out of Marylebone, the 'Pennine Pullman' called at Sheffield over the Pennines and back up the East Coast main line. No. 60014 **Silver Link** is about to enter Catesby tunnel travelling at just under 60 m.p.h. having shut off steam for a P.W. slack.

12 May 1956

92 Following the 'Pennine Pullman' was a service train headed by No. 60063 **Isinglass** and about to pass through Charwelton station. Many of the Great Central stations were sited between the running lines and you will notice here the lines opening out to allow room for the platform.

12 May 1956

93 The 'Cornishman' ran from Wolverhampton to Penzance in both directions. The train from Wolverhampton is shown here coming off the west triangle at Hatton behind No. 5070 **Sir Daniel Gooch**. The line to the right goes to Hatton station and on to Leamington. The west triangle has now been singled as has the branch as far as Bearley.

15 May 1956

94

The fastest train in the book ends this volume in the middle of 1956. I am sure No. 7030 **Cranbrook Castle** was travelling at over 70 m.p.h. as it passes Ruscombe halfway between Maidenhead and Reading. The train is of course the down 'Bristolian'.

22 May 1956